An Introduction to First & Second Thessalonians
The Message of Christ in Turmoil and Tranquility

First Fruits Press
The Academic Open Press of Asbury Theological Seminary
859-858-2236
first.fruits@asburyseminary.edu
http://place.asburyseminary.edu/firstfruits

Asbury Theological Seminary
204 N. Lexington Ave., Wilmore, KY 40390
asburyseminary.edu
800-2ASBURY

An Introduction to First & Second Thessalonians: The Message of Christ in Turmoil and Tranquility: A Formational and Theological Interpretation by R. Jeffrey Hiatt.

Published by First Fruits Press, © 2014

Digital version at http://place.asburyseminary.edu/academicbooks/7/

For all other uses, contact First Fruits Press:
859-858-2236
first.fruits@asburyseminary.edu

ISBN: 9781621711186 (Print), 9781621711520 (Digital)

Hiatt, R. Jeffrey (Robert Jeffrey)
An introduction to first and second Thessalonians: the message of Christ in turmoil and tranquility, by R. Jeffrey Hiatt.
ix, 97 p. : ill., fascims, map ; 21 cm.
Wilmore, Ky. : First Fruits Press, c2014.
Includes biblical references
ISBN: 9781621711186 (pbk.)
1. Bible – Thessalonians – Commentaries. I. Title.
BS2725.53 .H34 2014   227.81077

Cover design by Kelli Dierdorf

An Introduction to

First & Second
thessalonians
The Message of Christ in
Turmoil and Tranquility

*A Formational and
Theological Interpretation*

by

R. Jeffrey Hiatt

*First Fruits Press
Wilmore, Ky
c2014*

Dedication

Beulah Florence Moore (Adams)
1894 – 1982

Beloved grandmother, who exemplified entire sanctification by her life lived for others. Her kindness and gentleness in words, actions, and gifts offered to her family, church, friends and strangers continually revealed the love of Jesus in her life.

Table of Contents

2 Thessalonians

Christian Formation Exercises

v

Word's from the Author

This work is intended to be an introduction for students and lay persons interested in a scholarly informed, but easily accessible, biblical study for personal or small group Christian formation. For technical scholarly arguments debating the variants, intricacies of nuanced interpretation, conclusions and decisions regarding the selection of each of the elements and its details, refer to the sources cited and their bibliographies.

Biblical translations are my own interpretation of scripture following the Nestle's Greek text and consulting with the NRSV, NASB, and NIV versions of the Bible.

Acknowledgments

Many people and scholars have poured hours of teaching and godly example into this effort. Their skills and dedication have converged to inspire this theological and formational exercise. Hal A. Cauthron taught me how to read Scripture with passion. Alvin Lawhead inspired me to listen to the Old Testament prophets speak from their own time and context. Alex R. G. Deasley and Morris Weigelt shaped my understanding and interpretation of the New Testament biblical texts. H. Ray Dunning, Rob L. Staples and William M. Greathouse guided my theological formation under God's watchful eye. Don W. Dunnington and Dee Freeborn provided pastoral and formational counsel and guidance. To each of these doctors of the Church and experts of their disciplines, I offer my gratitude; I honor them for each of these gifts.

General Overview of Thessalonians

Context

Ancient Thessalonica[1] was an important center of Greek influence. It was founded in 315 A.D. by King Cassander (also spelled Kassander) and named for his wife, the half-sister of Alexander the Great. Since Thessalonica allied itself with the winners in the Second Civil War of Rome, Antony and Octavius, it was granted political status and made a "free city"[2] (Acts 17:6). Thessalonica was located on the main (Egnatian) highway between the East and West, was the largest Macedonian city, had a famous harbor,[3] and was a thriving center of culture (Greeks, Jews, and others) and commerce. Due to its central location and influence, Thessalonica became a key center in the Roman Empire and for Christian missionary strategy.[4]

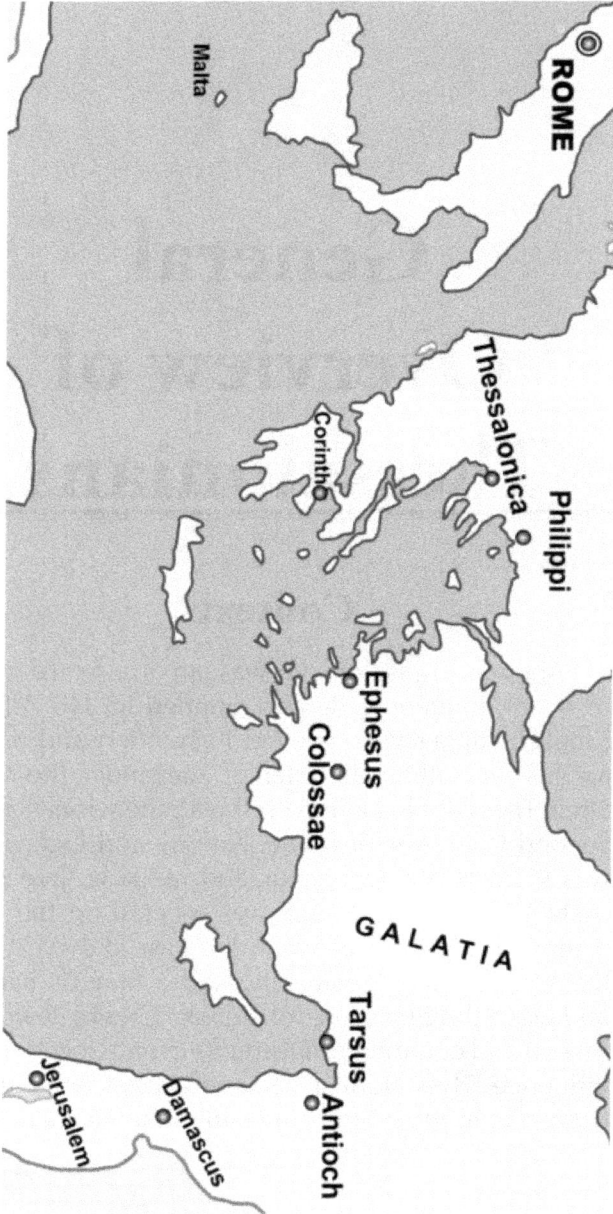

Image 1: Geographic map of Europe during Paul of Tarsus' times.

Author and Recipients

Paul, his co-workers, and traveling companions crossed the Aegean Sea from Troas and landed in Macedonia, selecting Thessalonica as a strategic center for the work of the church, and igniting the Christian missionary movement into Europe (Acts 16:6-12). By the time Paul, Silas and Timothy[5] had to leave Thessalonica due to persecution and a death threat against Paul, a thriving and faithful group of a few Jews and some Greeks (who had been won over from paganism) were able to carry on the Christian witness in that area (Cf. 1 Thessalonians 1:9, 2:14; Acts 14:15, 15:19, 17:1-10).[6]

Place, Date and Occasion for Writing

Paul then went to Beroea, Athens, and Corinth, having somewhat similar results.[7] He preached in the synagogues, witnessed to the people, and established churches, all while being pursued by his persecutors (cf. Acts 17:1-15)! Paul felt uneasy about leaving the

Image 2: Stater (or silver coin) of Cassander, the founder of Thessalonica.

new church at Thessalonica, and sent Timothy back to check on their well being. When Timothy came back with a good report, Paul, happy to hear the encouraging news, sent the letters we call 1 and 2 Thessalonians from Corinth in the spring of A.D. 50 (or 51) as a follow-up to address important issues in the lives of the young believers.[8]

Image 3: Painting by Rembrandt of Paul.

Overview of Themes and Significance

The contents of these letters overflow with love and encouragement. Paul writes to them as a father would write to his family and close friends. He tenderly talks of his relationship with them and his concern for their welfare. He praises them for even the smallest gains in their lives as Christians. He disciplines them for their failures and shortcomings as he urges them to make the changes needed to become mature, honorable Christians.[9]

Image 4: View looking south from the upper city of Thessaloniki. The snow-covered peaks in the distance are those of Mt. Olympus, the highest mountain in Greece, southwest of Thessaloniki. Boats in the port of Thessaloniki can be seen and the buildings of the modern city are also visible.

The 1 Thessalonians letter expresses four main concerns:

1) Paul and the ministry were being slandered by his enemies
2) Some members were tempted to moral laxity;
3) Part of the group misunderstood Jesus' Second Coming
4) A few were disregarding church leadership and discipline.

Paul confronts these issues, especially by urging Christian formation in heart holiness and growth in grace (1 Thessalonians 5:23-24). In 2 Thessalonians, the first two problems mentioned above were mostly resolved, but issues three and four still needed more comment (see 2 Thessalonians 2:1-3 starting on page 52 and 13-17 starting on page 53). Paul also wrote to encourage those who were facing persecution.[10]

This first letter of Paul is recognized as the beginning of the New Testament.[11] Paul writes decisively on some of the church's most important doctrines: the deity of Christ, the Holy Spirit, sanctification of believers, and Christ's Second Coming. In these two letters, we see the heart of the veteran missionary as he guides and inspires the fledgling churches and the whole Christian movement under the direction of the Holy Spirit.

The second letter to the Thessalonians gives more of an emphasis to the latter two themes of the *Parousia* of Christ referred to in problem three, and church discipline, mentioned above in the fourth problem, since these issues were not fully dealt with in the interlude between the two letters. Paul addressed the anxieties running through the community and also pointed to the wholeness and peace that is available in Christ. Thus, he is moving through the letter's sections, dealing with the turmoil, and pointing his readers to God's tranquility available in their daily lives.

The words found in these two short books of the New Testament give the reader descriptions, warnings, advice, and inspiration concerning God's gracious dealing with his people.[12] The reader will find many of Paul's more elaborate doctrines found in his other epistles here in a more rudimentary form. Yet, he says more about his understanding of Christ's return within these pages. God extends an invitation to each reader to be a part of this exciting, growing community. You are invited, too!

Structure of Thessalonians

Paul penned his letters using an ancient standard form of logic to present important ideas along with their supporting evidence, and followed by a conclusion. Fredrick J. Long suggests this form of logic follows this outline:
1) Major Premise *(propositio)*
2) Proof of Major Premise *(propositionis approbatio)*
3) Minor Premise *(assumptio)*
4) Proof of Minor Premise *(assumptionis approbatio)*
5) Conclusion *(cone/usio)*[13]

Although Paul may have used this form of logic to organize the ideas and information, it should not be construed as a scheming technique of rhetoric to persuade by manipulation, but rather an ordered way of communicating to help his readers/hearers follow his message and reasoning.[14] Thus, I will deal with the content of the letters with the above mentioned structure and themes in mind. Yet, the emphasis of the interpretation will be placed on the formational and theological implications of the material.

Overview of 2 Thessalonians

This letter beams with love and encouragement like 1 Thessalonians. Two other guiding underlying themes emerge and run as interwoven dialog partners whose voices can be heard throughout the letter: turmoil and tranquility. These actual words are not used in the letter, as such, but their fingerprints are visible on nearly every verse.

The 2 Thessalonians letter expresses the same sentiments as 1 Thessalonians, but Paul does not mention that he and the ministry were being slandered by his enemies. He only briefly mentioned the issue of temptation to moral laxity. Paul spent the bulk of his instruction addressing the misunderstandings concerning Jesus' Second Coming and the devaluing of church leadership and discipline by some of the Thessalonian believers.

Thus, Paul deepened his teachings concerning the Second Coming of Christ to allay the misconceptions and practices of those who were still in error about this important aspect of the Christian faith. He indicated that he suspected that some of the trouble was stirred up from a false letter purporting to be from him.[33] Paul pointed out that certain "signs" must happen before

Christ returns (2:3-12) in order to put an end to the laziness of some of their number. That is, some of the Thessalonians were just sitting around "watching and waiting," and spreading idle gossip! Paul encouraged them to be faithful by continuing their appropriate daily activities and responsibilities, demonstrating the love and grace of Christ before a watching world around them.

Image 5: The excavations of the Forum/Agora in Thessaloniki. The arched structures are part of the lower portion of the forum. The columns are located on the upper portion of the forum. This may have been the area of the "marketplace" where a mob started to riot in the city (Acts 17: 5) due to the preaching of Paul and Silas.

14 ✝Luke the beloued physician greeteth you, and Demas.

15 Salute the brethren which are of Laodicea, and Nymphas, & the Church which is in his house.

16 And when this Epistle is read of you, cause that it be read in the Church of the Laodiceans also, and that yee likewise reade the Epistle *written from Laodicea.*

17 And say to Archippus, Take heed to the ministerie, that thou hast receiued in the Lord, that thou fulfill it.

18 The salutation by the hand of me Paul. Remember my bands. Grace *be* with you. Amen.

¶ Written from Rome to the Colossians, *and sent by Tychicus, and Onesimus.*

THE FIRST EPISTLE OF
PAVL TO THE THES-
SALONIANS.

CHAP. I.

Aul, and Siluanus, and Timotheus, vnto the Church of the Thessalonians, *which is* in God the Father, and in the Lord Iesus Christ: Grace *be* with you, & peace from God our Father, and *from* the Lord Iesus Christ.

2 We giue God thankes alwayes for you all, making mention of you in our prayers

3 Without ceasing, remembring your effectuall faith, and diligent loue, and the patience of *your* hope in our Lord Iesus Christ, in the sight of God, euen our Father,

4 Knowing, beloued brethren, that ye are elect of God.

CHAP. II.

1 thessalonians

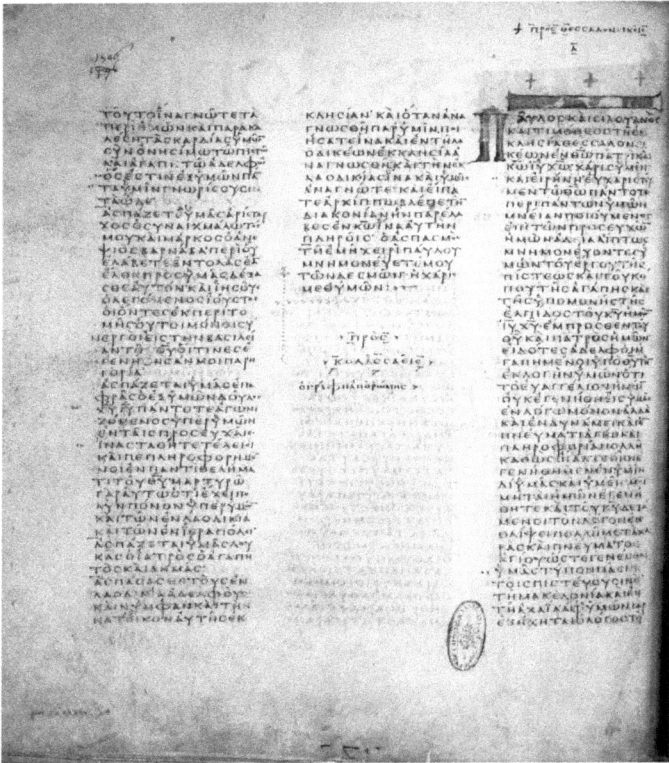

Image 7: The Greek text of Colossians
4:7-18 and 1 Thessalonians 1:1-8 from
the Codex Vaticanus B (pg. 1506).

Book Outline

I. Faith Working by Love (1:1-3:13)
  A. The Ministry of the Gospel and Paul
    1. Salutation (1:1)
    2. The Thessalonians' Faith
       and Example (1:2-10)
    3. Paul's Ministry Among the
       Thessalonians (2:1-16)
  B. Paul's Pastoral Concerns (2:17-3:13)
    1. Spiritual Safety and Witness (2:17-20)
    2. Timothy's Mission (3:1-5)
    3. Timothy's Report of Faithfulness (3:6-8)
    4. Paul's Reactions and Prayer (3:9-13)
II. Blameless at Jesus' Coming (4:1-5:28)
  A. Exhortation to Christian Living (4:1-12)
    1. Live to Please God (4:1-2)
    2. Avoid Sexual Sin (4:3-8)
    3. Love One Another (4:9-12)
  B. Jesus' Second Coming (4:13-5:11)
    1. The Dead in Christ (4:13-18)
    2. The Day of the Lord (5:1-11)
  C. Christian Leadership and Discipline (5:12-22)
    1. Esteem Leaders and Accept
       Discipline (5:12-15)
    2. Attitude of Holiness (5:16-18)
    3. Spiritual Discernment (5:19-22)
  D. Closing Prayer and Comments (5:23-28)
    1. Prayer for Entire Sanctification (5:23-24)
    2. Final Instructions (5:25-28)

I. Faith Working by Love (1:1-3:13)

Paul was a theologian and missionary on the move. He had to travel lightly and be aware of his pursuers who would end his life if the opportunity presented itself. Paul did not live in fear. Instead he lived by a faith characterized and grounded in God's love for him. Paul wanted to convey this love and faith to his listeners. What God had done for him, Christ would do for them, too. The Spirit present with Paul was the same Holy Spirit available to all. These words are still true for Jesus' followers today.

A. The Ministry of the Gospel and Paul

1 Paul, Silas,[15] and Timothy, to the church of the Thessalonians in God the Father and the Lord Jesus Christ: Grace to you and peace.

²We give thanks to God always for you all, mentioning *you* in our prayers, ceaselessly; ³before our God and Father we remember your work *by* faith, and labor of love, and steadfast hope in our Lord Jesus Christ.
◇◇◇

1. Salutation (1:1)

At the beginning of Paul's correspondence to the churches under his ministry, he conveyed the essence (grace and peace)[16] of the blessing of Israel found in Numbers 6:23-26 to his readers. Paul establishes the character and nature of what he says by grounding it in "God the Father and the Lord Jesus Christ" (1:1) and in the Spirit. "[O]ur gospel came to you not only in word, but also in power and in the Holy Spirit and with full conviction" (1:5). "The Spirit is understood as the power and presence of God (Shekinah),[17] functioning as the life-giving agent in the age of the Kingdom."[18]

2. The Thessalonians' Faith and Example (1:2-10)

◇◇◇

4 You know, brothers and sisters,[19] beloved by God, He chose you, ⁵because our gospel came to you not only in word, but in power, in the Holy Spirit and with full conviction; as you know, our lives among you were consistent with the gospel for your sake. ⁶And you

became imitators of us and of the Lord, despite persecution, welcoming the word with joy in the Holy Spirit, [7]so that you became a pattern to all of the believers throughout Macedonia and Achaia. [8]For from you the word of the Lord has rung out beyond Macedonia and Achaia to everywhere we have been, so that we have no need to speak about it. [9]Travelers in the region keep reporting the news about the wonderful welcome we had among you, and how you converted from idols to serve the living and true God, [10]and to wait for His Son from heaven, whom He raised from the dead, Jesus, who is the one to deliver us from the coming wrath.

Paul heaped high praise upon his first readers as he wrote these words to them. Not only had he blessed them with a lofty blessing, but he referred to them with a name that was usually reserved by the Jews for great men, like Moses, or Solomon, or for the nation of Israel itself: "beloved of God!"[20] Paul was trying to convey their high status in the eyes of God because of their being "in Christ."

Paul's own faith, faithfulness, and Christ-like character (see 2:1-16 starting on page 18) displayed the gospel's power as an example to the Thessalonians. They noted that what Paul said matched the way he lived. This was in contrast to other itinerant teachers of novel philosophies who passed through town, trying to garner followers to support them financially. Thus, they listened to Paul and "received the word with joy inspired by the Holy Spirit" (1:6). Christ-like character must be produced in the life of believers, disciples, and all true Christians.

The Thessalonians faith and Christian example was so evident in their changed lives that not only did they become the talk of the town, but the whole region of Greece knew of their faith in Christ (1:7-8). Paul noted that they had become a model church. They were remaining strong in the face of crushing pressure and maintaining their joy in the Lord. Their witness for the Lord strategically traveled both east toward Asia and west toward Rome, advancing Christianity as a contender among the world religions. They had turned from paganism, worshiping "idols, to serve a living and true God" (1:9). This upset some of the other local people. In this central life-change, Paul affirmed their decision and their faithful conduct to follow the Lord, anticipating Christ's return and His rescue of those who trust Him (1:10).

Paul introduces the famous triad of Christian character: faith, love and hope, and commends their solid expression of each in their conduct. This is noted by their active faith, labor that expresses love, and the patient endurance because of hope in "our Lord Jesus Christ"(1:3).[21] Paul later wrote of "faith working by love," (Galatians 5:6) which became the trademark of John Wesley's ministry in the eighteenth century. The Thessalonian converts exhibited these Christian hallmarks as evidence of their appointment by God to be part of those who take up the responsibility of God's mission and witness to their faith in Christ to all who will listen (1:4-10).

3. Paul's Ministry Among the Thessalonians (2:1-16)

◇◇◇

2 You know, brothers and sisters, that our visit to you was not a failure. [2]We had previously suffered and been maligned in Philippi, as you know, but boldly with the help of our God, we spoke his gospel to you, in spite of strong opposition. [3]For our preaching did not spring from deceit, or impure motives, or trickery. [4]Instead, we speak as those approved by God to be entrusted with the gospel. We are not trying to please people but God, who proves the motives or our hearts. [5]As you know, and God is our witness, we never used flattery, nor any pretext for greed [6]nor praise from people, not from you or anyone else, [7]even though we could have asserted our authority as apostles of Christ. Instead, we were gentle among you.

Just as a nursing mother cherishes her children, [8]so we cared for you. Because we loved you so much, we were delighted to share with you not only the gospel of God but our lives as well. [9]You remember, brothers and sisters, our toil and labor; we worked night and day in order not to burden to anyone while we preached the gospel of God to you. [10]You are witnesses, and God also, of how holy, righteous and blameless we were among you who believed. [11] For you know that we dealt with each of you like a father deals with his children, [12] encouraging, comforting and urging you to live lives worthy of God, who calls you into his kingdom and glory.

[13] And we also thank God continually because, when you received the word of God, which you heard from us, you accepted it not as a human word, but as it actually is, the word of God, which is indeed at work in you who believe. [14] For you, brothers and sisters, became imitators of God's churches in Judea, which are in Christ Jesus: You suffered from your own countrymen the same things those churches suffered from the Jews [15] who killed the Lord Jesus and the prophets and also chased us out; they displease God and oppose everyone [16] by their efforts to hinder us from speaking to the Gentiles so that they may be saved. Thus, they are piling up their sins to the limit, but God's wrath has come upon them at last.

Paul was not writing for sentiment or nostalgia. He was defending his character and the integrity of the gospel. All three men were there to preach and live out the gospel, not to be idle or try to live off of the Thessalonians (2:1). They did not come with motives of trickery or deceit. Their aim to give the Good News of Christ to the nations was amply rewarded by the Thessalonians' changed lives. They had become true believers, giving witness to Christ so strongly, even in the face of persecution, that their reputation of changed lives was being talked about abroad, affirming that the mission of Paul and his associates among the Thessalonians was effective and from godly intentions, instead of human designs (2: 3, 5, 8, 10, 13, 16).

In fact, Paul had been so gentle among them that he treated them like his own family, caring for them, producing his own financial support, and sharing not only God's Word with them, but also his own personal life (2:7, 9, 11-12). Although the Thessalonians were persecuted, they were in good company with Paul and his co-workers, the prophets of old, and even the Lord Himself (2:15). God honored the Thessalonians with His salvation and was bringing His wrath on their persecutors (2:14, 16). Because of what God had done, and was continuing to do in Thessalonica, Paul continually gave thanks for them (2:13).

Paul's mood stiffens, however, when he considers what is ahead for their persecutors. When 2:15-16 is taken in light of Romans 2, Philippians 3:1-7, and Romans 9-11, Paul is keenly aware of the mission of the Jews, their privileges and responsibilities, and he sees that their sins are egregious and destructive. Paul feels the weight of love for them in spite of their evil actions, so he sternly warns of the high cost of religion without love.[22]

B. Paul's Pastoral Concerns (2:17-3:13)

◇◇

[17]But we, brothers and sisters, were bereaved for a short time of your presence,

but not in our hearts, and we took all the more pains in much love to see your faces. [18]And we wished to come to you, I Paul, again and again, but Satan hindered me. [19]For what is our hope [of honor] and our joy and crowning achievement, but you alone, before our Lord Jesus at his coming? [20]For you are our glory and our joy.

3 Therefore when we could stand it no longer, we thought it best to be left by ourselves in Athens. [2]We sent Timothy, who is our brother and God's co-worker in proclaiming the gospel of Christ, to strengthen and encourage you in your faith, [3]so that no one would be sidelined by these persecutions. You know quite well that we were appointed for them. [4]In fact, when we were with you, we told you that we would be persecuted. And it turned out that way, as you well know. [5]For this reason, when I could bear it no longer, I sent to find out about your faith. I was concerned that in some way the tempter might have gotten the best of you and our efforts might have been voided.

[6]But Timothy has just now come to us from you and has brought to us good news about your faith and love. He has told us that you always have fond memories of us and that you long to see us, just as we also long to see you. [7]Therefore, brothers and sisters, during all our distress and persecution we have been encouraged about you because of your faith; [8]because it enlivens us, if

you stand firm in the Lord. [9]How can we thank God enough for you in return for all the joy we have in the presence of our God because of you? [10]Night and day we pray most earnestly for you, and ask that we may see you again to help you with any shortcoming in your faith.

[11]Now may our God and Father himself and our Lord Jesus direct our way to come to you. [12]May the Lord make your love increase and overflow for each other and for everyone else, just as ours does for you. [13]May he strengthen your hearts so that you will be blameless and holy in the presence of our God and Father when our Lord Jesus comes with all his holy ones.[23]

Paul had to leave the Thessalonians, but his thoughts and heart were ever turning toward them. Paul longed to know what had happened to them since his forced departure. Since Paul was prevented from going back to them right away, he had to discover the answer another way.

1. Spiritual Safety and Witness (2:17-20)

Paul's pastoral heart is laid bare as he pours out his deep concern for them. He may have been chased away from them recently, but his desire to be with them intensified. They not only converted to Christ under his care, but were precious to him personally.

Although his attackers accused him of pretending concern, Paul adamantly maintains his devotion to them as a shepherd who tenderly cares for his flock. They and their well-being in the faith, constantly weighed on his heart (2:17-18).

The Thessalonians were a shining testimony that Paul's work counted for something more precious than financial gain or fame. They were a point of hope, but especially a joy to his heart. Love rejoices in the good and triumph of others. Their faith in Christ was an evidence of both God's work and a validation of Paul's legitimate ministry claims. They were the proof that he was not a fraud, because their lives displayed the power of the gospel to transform lives. Thus, Paul was happy about the grace at work in their lives (2:19-20).

2. Timothy's Mission (3:1-5)

Paul's anxiety over the state of their souls, however, compelled him to dispatch Timothy to see about them. Paul was uncertain if persecution might have caused them to turn away from Christ. If they were lost to the tempter, Paul's work would have been voided there (3:1-5). Paul wanted to see them weather the storms of tribulation. His love for them and the gospel were on the line. Paul wanted them to know that they were not alone, not forgotten. There is help in the time of trouble.

3. Timothy's Report of Faithfulness (3:6-8)

Timothy conveyed Paul's deep love for them, and upon Timothy's return to Paul, he brought the news that Paul hoped to hear. The Thessalonians were holding firm through their difficulties, and their thoughts were as much about Paul as his were about them. Their feelings toward one another were mutual. Holy love had carried the day! Both Paul and the Thessalonians were comforted by Timothy's trip (3:6-8).

4. Paul's Reactions and Prayer (3:9-13)

What joy fills the soul when our friends are faithful! Paul rejoices and gives thanks[24] to God not only for the Thessalonians and for what their lives mean to him personally, but also for the work of the church. Their radiant example spurs him to pray for them night and day to excel still more and to press on to a more complete life in Christ. There is still much for them to learn, and Paul longs to be a part of completing their education and spiritual growth in Christ (3:9-10).

Paul's goal for them to be full in Christ comes through as he penned this part of his prayer to show his open heart. He longed for them to overflow in the love of Christ for one another and to reach out beyond their surroundings to other groups of people in the same love (3:11-12). In this exultant prayer, Paul struck this high note of connecting heart holiness to being prepared to meet Christ and His attendants[25] on the day of Christ's return (*parusia*) (3:13). In short, love, holiness, and mission are inseparable. They are linked to Christ's Second Coming as an "incentive to live and work in a manner worthy of Christ."[26]

Image 8: Saint Timothy Icon.

II. Blameless at Jesus' Coming (4:1-5:28)

If Paul can convey the importance of living by faith and love with an eye toward Jesus' return, then believers will hold onto the important truths of being a Christian. They can then live a consistent lifestyle that can rebuff any false accusations to the contrary. Being and doing reside in Christ-like faithfulness. This lofty goal may seem impossible to the casual Christian, but Paul explains how God makes it a reality in the life of "those who believe."

A. Exhortation to Christian Living (4:1-12)

4 Finally, dear brothers and sisters, we urge you in the Lord Jesus to live in a way that pleases God, as we have taught you. You are doing this, and we encourage you to do so even more. ²For

you know what we taught you by the authority of the Lord Jesus.

³God's will for you is to be holy, refrain from sexual sin. ⁴Then each of you will control his own body and live in sanctification and honor— ⁵not in lustful passion like the peoples who do not know God. ⁶Never mistreat a Christian brother or sister in this matter, for the Lord avenges all such sins, as we have solemnly warned you. ⁷God has not called us to impure lives, but to live holy lives. ⁸Therefore, anyone who refuses to live this way is not disobeying a human teaching but is rejecting God, who gives his Holy Spirit to you.

⁹But we do not need to write to you about loving each other, for God himself has taught you to love one another. ¹⁰Indeed, you already practice your love for all the believers throughout Macedonia. Even so, dear brothers and sisters, we exhort you to love them even more. ¹¹Aspire to live a quiet life, to mind your own matters, and to work with your hands—just as we instructed you previously. ¹²Then you may live prudently among non-Christians and will not be dependent on others.

As Paul moves into the second half of the letter, he focuses on some of the practical concerns of living as a Christian, exhorting his readers to live according to scriptural holiness, godly love in action. In the first half of the letter, Paul laid the foundation for these exhortations. He gave the supporting ideas and evidence for the conclusions and directives which follow.

1. Live to Please God (4:1-2)

Paul did not merely make a suggestion, but reminded the Thessalonians of the importance of pleasing God (4:1). Although this is in command form, it is bound by the cords of love. These constraints are pleasant ties that hold the heart captive, not from force, but by willing participation. Relationships have boundaries and guidelines. God defines the type of relationships allowed and what actions are appropriate to each type of relationship (4:2). Humans abandon these established relationships at their own peril.

2. Avoid Sexual Sin (4:3-8)

Paul addressed one of the deepest challenges to our human relations when he covered appropriate behavior associated with our sexuality. He forbade animal-like behaviors and any actions which exploited anyone on the basis of this vulnerable and deeply personal aspect of our lives. People are not objects to be misused for our own personal gain or whims.

As image-bearers of God, we are created to reflect a godlike character in our whole lives. We do not compartmentalize different portions, or wall off one part of who we are from other facets. To participate in fornication, adultery, or any sexual vice is to defile the whole life, and Paul enumerates a list of unacceptable behaviors in other later letters (see Galatians 5:19;

Ephesians 3:3-5; Colossians 3:3-5; 1 Corinthians 5:1, 6:9-10; 2 Corinthians 12:21).[27] In this first correspondence, Paul remembered that the prevailing culture surrounding them and the area where they lived offered a great amount of temptation because of the sexual profligacy pervasive in the pagan worship practices in their city (4:3-8).

The Thessalonians were shown a higher life. A life of purity and holy love, not lust or sexual misconduct, was to characterize their reputation. Paul's warning is that there is a strict judgment on those who violate another person at this deep level of their personhood. He reminded them that this does not originate with him, or any other human teacher, but from the LORD! This matter carries the highest form of retribution levied on one who commits these acts against the dignity of another. Anyone who disputes this is not rejecting the unwelcome advice of a critic, but a core divine teaching. This is no small rebuff and snubbing. It can have both temporal and eternal consequences. Beware! (4:7-8).

Paul taught the Thessalonians from both the negative and the positive side. He told them what to avoid - sexual immorality, and then what to pursue - holiness. God's grace is what makes this available to them, and they were invited to join in the sanctification of their lives. God will establish their hearts, and their lives will reflect the changes. Holy love will be its chief manifestation (refer 3:10-13; 4:9).[28]

3. Love One Another (4:9-12)

Paul was not, however, accusing the Thessalonians of this negative behavior. Just the opposite. They had been sterling examples of godly love toward each other and those across the region. People marveled at their magnanimous love. Their hospitality had become famous in the gossip circles. Who had not heard of their kindness? Paul commended them and urged them to excel even more! Love knows no end of growth (4:1, 9-11). The more love you give away, the more there is to give—like the bread passed among the crowd at the feeding of the 5,000!

Earlier in the letter, Paul established guidelines on how to tell what is good and how any true message in the Spirit should lead to virtue and holy living. This brings together the concepts of the Spirit, sanctification, and the ethical dimension.[29] Paul wed sanctification to the work of the Spirit and revealed the goal as the production of an ethical character, making people more like Christ (2:13).[30] The way this influences daily life also includes what kind of work they do. Paul does not specifically earmark certain professions, but his own trade allowed him to provide for his needs and share with others. He was not trying to make a living off of the gospel. He was not a "gospel peddler," as some attackers had already suggested. He was calling attention to the godly aspect of work as a means of grace, through which God provides for us and allows us to share with others. Paul taught them this way of life by his example and through his instruction (4:12).

B. Jesus' Second Coming (4:13-5:11)

◇◇

[13]Brothers and sisters, we do not want you to be uninformed about those who fall asleep, or to grieve like others do who have no hope. [14]We believe that Jesus died and arose to life again; we also believe that when Jesus returns, God will bring with Jesus those who have fallen asleep in him. [15]By the Lord's own word, we tell you that we who are still alive, who are left until the coming of the Lord, will certainly not precede those who have fallen asleep. [16]For the Lord himself will come down from heaven, with a loud summons, with the voice of the archangel and with the trumpet call of God, and the dead in Christ will rise first. [17]After that, we who are still alive and remain will be caught up together with them in the clouds will meet the Lord in the air and will be with the Lord always. [18]Therefore encourage each other with these words.

Now concerning the times and dates, brothers and sisters, we do not need to write to you, [2]for you know very well that the day of the Lord will come like a thief in the night. [3]While people are saying, "Peace and safety," destruction will come on them suddenly, as labor pains on a pregnant woman, and they will not escape.

⁴But you, beloved brothers and sisters, are not in the dark so that this day should surprise you like a thief. ⁵You are all children of the light and of the day. We do not belong to the night or to the darkness. ⁶So then, let us not be like others, who fall asleep, but let us be alert and self-controlled. ⁷For those who sleep, sleep at night, and those who get drunk, get drunk at night. ⁸But since we belong to the day, let us be self-controlled, putting on faith and love as a breastplate, and the hope of salvation as a helmet. ⁹For God did not appoint us to suffer wrath but to obtain salvation through our Lord Jesus Christ. ¹⁰He died for us so that, whether we are alive or dead, we may live together with him. ¹¹Therefore encourage one another and build each other up, just as in fact you are doing.

The doctrine on Christ's return (*Parousia*) is one of the most controversial aspects found in Christianity. Eschatological theories abound on how and when it will happen. Jesus foretells of His return, but gives only hints as to when it will be. Many people across the centuries have tried to pinpoint a year, and even a day, but they have all been wrong. If it is so important, why is it so mysterious? Although not many details are forthcoming, what is disclosed is that this happening is not done in obscurity. What is to be avoided is curious speculation. The prime message here is that Jesus *is* coming back and his followers will always be *with* Him!

1. The Dead in Christ (4:13-18)

Paul explained to the Thessalonians that when Jesus returns, "the dead in Christ will rise first," then the living Christians "will meet Jesus in the air with them" and His attendants (4:13-17). Paul's main purposes in telling the Thessalonians these things was: 1) to stir up their hope, averting despair because of grief for those who have died (4:13); 2) to alleviate any doubt about where those who are in Christ will spend eternity—*with Christ* (4:18). Everyone who puts their trust in Christ will not be disappointed.

2. The Day of the Lord (5:1-11)

The concept of the "day of the Lord" comes from ancient times and is associated with fear and judgment on Israel's enemies. Yet, it conveys hope and vindication for the people of God. Christ's return carries similar sentiments as well. For the faithful believer, it means hope that will be fulfilled. For the enemies of God, it is a catastrophic day of dread. We must be careful about who we assume are "enemies" of God.[31] It is more important that we look to our own soul when it comes to judging others. This concept calls for the personal question, "Am I ready to meet the Lord?"

Real Christians do not need to fear. Thus, they do not need to know the exact time of Jesus' arrival. Paul clarifies: be alert; keep awake; live a life of faith working by love devoted to Christ (5:6). They are not people of the darkness, stumbling through the night. The gospel is a lamp for their feet and a light along their path (Ps. 119:105). Christians are people of the light. They should encourage one another with this reminder (5:1, 5, 8, 11). Christians are people of servanthood, who live by and offer the good news to others by losing their life for Christ's sake, and, therefore, find (save) it (Matt. 16:25b).

In contrast, those who blindly assume that "all is well" have a rude awakening coming (5:3). The wrath of God will overtake them in their stupor, "like a thief in the night." Neglect of godliness and rejection of Christ will mark their destination. Their end is explained ahead of time as incurring God's wrath and facing an inescapable destruction (5:3, 7, 9). These are people who are trying to selfishly preserve their life for their own sake, and will therefore lose it (Matthew 16:25a).

C. Christian Leadership and Discipline (5:12-22)

◇◇

[12]Now we ask you, brothers and sisters, to respect those who work among you, who lead you in the Lord and who admonish you. [13]Hold them in high esteem because of their work in love. Be at peace with each other. [14]And we urge you, brothers and sisters, warn those who are idle, encourage the timid, help the weak, be patient with them all. [15]Make sure that nobody pays back evil for evil, but always seek to do good to each other and to everyone else.

¹⁶Be joyful always; ¹⁷pray without ceasing; ¹⁸give thanks in all circumstances, for this is God's will for you in Christ Jesus.

¹⁹Do not stifle the Spirit; ²⁰do not treat prophecies with contempt. ²¹Sift everything that is said. Hold on to the good. ²²Avoid every kind of evil.

◇◇◇

In the moral light of Jesus' return, Paul continued to instruct the believers in Christian principles and actions. The consistency of the Christian life is reflected in its leadership and discipline. The point is that Christians need the fellowship of other Christians to thrive. The Bible knows of no solitary Christians, said Wesley. Communion with other believers is essential to the Christian life. This is what Wesley meant by "social holiness." We learn, practice, and grow in Christlikeness in fellowship with other Christians.

The Christian life is to be more than just, "me & Jesus." In fact, to state it more strongly, we need each other to be Christian. Without Christian fellowship others might lead us astray from the true faith. We can easily follow our own private ideas or make up our own religion, if we are left to ourselves.

1. Esteem Leaders and Accept Discipline (5:12-15)

Paul reminds the Thessalonians that leadership in the Church among believers carries the added responsibilities of nurturing others in the faith, guiding worship activities, helping to feed the poor, working for a living, and caring for those who cannot care for themselves. All of these labors of love call for respect, honor, and assistance, especially from other Christians (5:12-13).

We understand that it is hard to criticize your peers when they stray, but love constrains us as a faithful witness, and reminds us to be a true Christian friend. Paul reminded them to "esteem highly" and listen to those who act in love with the courage and the spiritual wisdom to reprove wrong behavior or false teachings (5:14-15).

2. Attitude of Holiness (5:16-18)

God's will is that our attitude toward Christian work be rooted in: the joy of the Lord, the habit of prayer, submitting all things to the Lord's guidance, and gratitude as a way of life. Paul exemplified this attitude of gratitude before the Thessalonians. He was thankful for them, to them, about them, and among them!

John Wesley often used these three verses to describe what the entirely sanctified life looked like on the face of a real Christian. Circumstances do not dictate our attitude, but our foundation in Christ is the foundation of our disposition (5:16-18). These characteristics display our true attitude in relation to God. It is a little like flying an airplane. If we want to fly well, these characteristics are like the control panel instruments which keep us level and heading into God's will, regardless of the turbulence around us.

3. Spiritual Discernment (5:19-22)

Paul admonished the Christian believers not to just accept anything that someone might attribute to "the Spirit." They should discern if what is said agrees with Christian principles, teachings, and revealed virtues. Although they are not to "despise prophetic utterances," and should "not quench [or repudiate] the Spirit" (5:19-20), they should "test" what is said, and "hold fast to that which is good" (5:21).

If we are respecting our leaders and holding them in loving esteem, if we are keeping our minds focused on and guided by God through prayer, letting joy stand guard over our heart, and embrace gratitude as our attitude, then we will not fall into doing evil either to other believers, or even to those who persecute us. Thus, we can avoid every kind of evil (5:19-22). With this, Paul set up the pinnacle of the letter in the closing prayer for the Thessalonians and subsequent Christian disciples.

D. Closing Prayer and Comments (5:23-28)

◇◇◇

²³May God himself, the God of peace, sanctify you entirely. May your whole spirit, soul, and body be kept blameless at the coming of our Lord Jesus Christ. ²⁴The one who calls you is faithful and he will do it.

²⁵Brothers and sisters, pray for us. ²⁶Greet all the believers with a holy kiss. ²⁷I charge you before the Lord to have this letter read to all the brothers and sisters.

²⁸The grace of our Lord Jesus Christ be with you.

∞∞∞∞∞∞∞∞∞∞∞∞∞∞∞∞∞∞∞∞∞∞∞∞∞∞∞∞∞∞∞∞

All that Paul has said to the church in the earlier lines of his letter comes to a dénouement in this section of the letter, particularly in verses 5:23-24. Everything Paul has described and prescribed for their behavior, attitudes, words, and thoughts can be embedded and empowered in this prayer. God will answer this prayer for any disciple who dares to pray it. Grace has motivated it. Courage calls us to step up and become the Christians that God wants us to be. Here is where we see the image of God restored in the heart of the believer. It is not just a promise *in* heaven; it is a necessary present preparation *for* heaven and fruitful ministry *on* earth.

1. Prayer for Entire Sanctification (5:23-24)

This personal heart-felt prayer stands behind the mission of Christian evangelism, discipleship, catechesis, life, and lifestyle as characterized by God's own essence. When love is enthroned in the heart, our alignment with the will and mission of God becomes single-minded.

This does not guarantee that all of our future performance will measure up to the model of Christ

Jesus, but it does insure that our intention will be guided by the motivations of godliness. It does indicate that we will accelerate in our growth in Christlikeness. It means that God has not only prepared our heart for His coming, but we are now ready to live "on earth as it is in heaven" in the sense of spiritual virtue, vitality, and what we value. It does not mean that we have arrived at the final destination in our Christian walk and can quit growing. That would lead in the opposite direction, away from Christ. No, it means that we are enabled to run the race set before us, disentangling ourselves from all that encumbers us. We can sprint to win the prize in Christ Jesus.

The indwelling of the Holy Spirit will give us "the mind of Christ." He will produce the "fruit of the Spirit" in us (Galatians 5:23-24). God himself will guard our heart. He will give us the gifts of the Spirit for ministry. He will operate the kingdom of God in us and through us. This high-watermark of the grace of God in the life of the Christian is the accelerated beginning of perfected love[32] to be lived out in the theater of the world (2 Corinthians 12:9). The deep gladness of the Father intersects our life through the work of the Son, enacted in and through us by the presence of the Holy Spirit for the work of ministry in the world.

The Christian does not boast of an elite privilege of power over others, but in humility we take up the towel of service to wash dirty feet, heal the sick, open the eyes of the blind, cause the lame to walk, the hungry to be fed, the naked to be clothed, and the good news of God's favor to be proclaimed across the globe. This is the power to release those held in captivity to sin. It casts out demons. It brings jobs to the unemployed. It drills wells of water in the desert. It educates. It gives a home to orphans, and provides for widows.

The peace that passes understanding adorns our head, heart, and hands as we become blameless before God. We become wholly his, "through and through," not by our own doing, but by God's faithful work in us by grace through faith. We become safe people, not out to exploit others, but concerned to do God's will in all settings, both among other believers, and also among those whose faith is lacking (5:23-24).

2. Final Instructions (5:25-28)

In Paul's final words of the letter, he reminds us that no one is above the need of prayer. In the fellowship of the church, we should pray for one another and especially for our leaders (5:25). The appropriate Christian greeting of recognition and the symbol of familial love should be exchanged among the believers to express our unity in Christ (5:26). The letter itself has a lasting value in the life of the church, both then and now, and should still be read to all the churches (5:27). From first to last, nothing can rise higher than the appropriated grace of Christ. All that we are or do is because God loved us and opened the way of salvation, divine favor to be poured out upon us, giving us every spiritual blessing in Christ (5:28). What will you do with this gift?

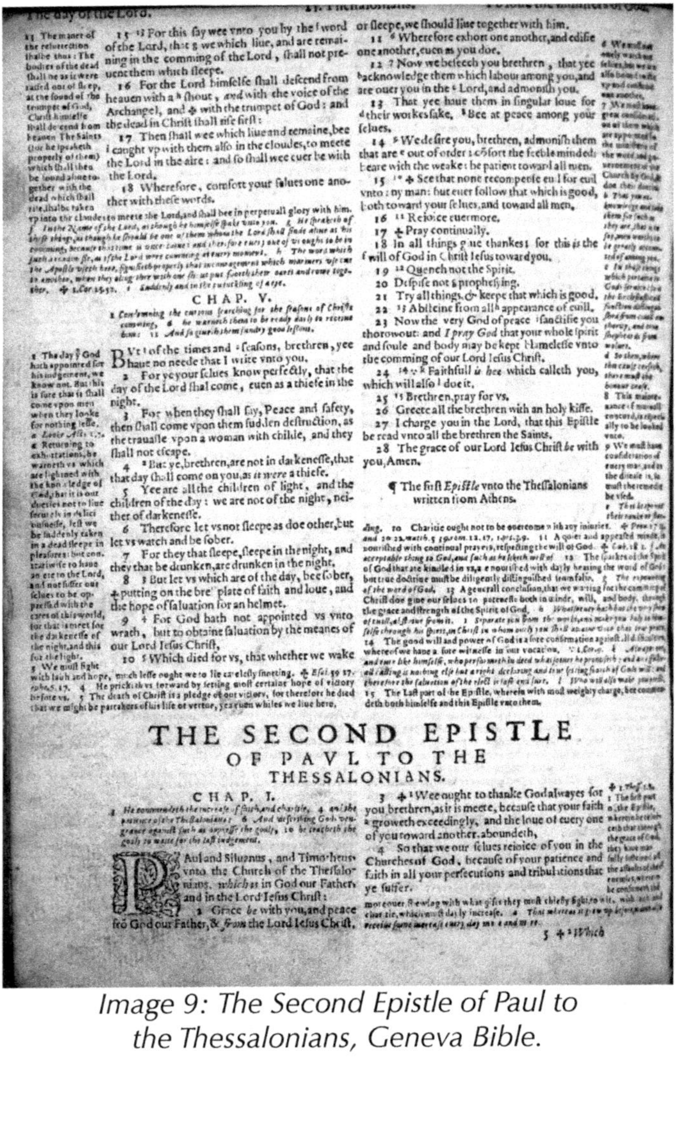
The day of the Lord.

15 For this say wee vnto you by the word of the Lord, that we which liue, and are remaining in the comming of the Lord, shall not preuent them which sleepe.

16 For the Lord himselfe shall descend from heauen with a shout, and with the voice of the Archangel, and with the trumpet of God: and the dead in Christ shall rise first:

17 Then shall wee which liue and remaine, bee caught vp with them also in the cloudes, to meete the Lord in the aire: and so shall wee euer be with the Lord.

18 Wherefore, comfort your selues one another with these words.

CHAP. V.

BVt of the times and seasons, brethren, yee haue no neede that I write vnto you.

2 For ye your selues know perfectly, that the day of the Lord shal come, euen as a thiefe in the night.

3 For when they shall say, Peace and safety, then shall come vpon them sudden destruction, as the trauaile vpon a woman with childe, and they shall not escape.

4 But ye, brethren, are not in darkenesse, that that day shall come on you, as it were a thiefe.

5 Yee are all the children of light, and the children of the day: we are not of the night, neither of darkenesse.

6 Therefore let vs not sleepe as doe other, but let vs watch and be sober.

7 For they that sleepe, sleepe in the night, and they that be drunken, are drunken in the night.

8 But let vs which are of the day, bee sober, putting on the brest plate of faith and loue, and the hope of saluation for an helmet.

9 For God hath not appointed vs vnto wrath, but to obtaine saluation by the meanes of our Lord Iesus Christ,

10 Which died for vs, that whether we wake or sleepe, we should liue together with him.

11 Wherefore exhort one another, and edifie one another, euen as you doe.

12 Now we beseech you brethren, that yee acknowledge them which labour among you, and are ouer you in the Lord, and admonish you.

13 That yee haue them in singular loue for their workes sake. Bee at peace among your selues.

14 We desire you, brethren, admonish them that are out of order: comfort the feeble minded: beare with the weake: be patient toward all men.

15 See that none recompense euil for euil vnto any man: but euer follow that which is good, both toward your selues, and toward all men.

16 Reioice euermore.

17 Pray continually.

18 In all things giue thankes: for this is the will of God in Christ Iesus toward you.

19 Quench not the Spirit.

20 Despise not prophesying.

21 Try all things, & keepe that which is good.

22 Absteine from all appearance of euill.

23 Now the very God of peace sanctifie you thorowout: and I pray God that your whole spirit and soule and body may be kept blamelesse vnto the comming of our Lord Iesus Christ.

24 Faithfull is hee which calleth you, which will also doe it.

25 Brethren, pray for vs.

26 Greete all the brethren with an holy kisse.

27 I charge you in the Lord, that this Epistle be read vnto all the brethren the Saints.

28 The grace of our Lord Iesus Christ be with you, Amen.

¶ The first Epistle vnto the Thessalonians written from Athens.

THE SECOND EPISTLE OF PAVL TO THE THESSALONIANS.

CHAP. I.

PAul and Siluanus, and Timotheus vnto the Church of the Thessalonians, which is in God our Father and in the Lord Iesus Christ:

2 Grace be with you, and peace frō God our Father, & from the Lord Iesus Christ.

3 Wee ought to thanke God alwayes for you brethren, as it is meete, because that your faith groweth exceedingly, and the loue of euery one of you toward another aboundeth,

4 So that we our selues reioice of you in the Churches of God, because of your patience and faith in all your persecutions and tribulations that ye suffer.

5 Which

Image 9: The Second Epistle of Paul to the Thessalonians, Geneva Bible.

2 Thessalonians

Image 10: The Greek text of 2 Thessalonians 3:11-18 and Hebrews 1:1-2:2 from the Codex Vaticanus B (pg. 1512).

Book Outline

I. Faith, Persecution, and Glory (1:1-12)
 A. Salutation (1:1-2)
 B. Thessalonian fidelity amid
   persecution (1:3-10)
 C. The glory of Christ at work in the
   Thessalonians (1:11-12)
**II. Turmoil and Tranquility: Teaching
 on the End Times (2:1-17)**
 A. Day of the Lord's Return (2:1-3)
 B. Rebellion and the Man of sin (2:4-12)
 C. Sanctification by the Spirit (2:13-15)
 D. Blessing of encouragement (2:16-17)
**III. Turmoil and Tranquility: Paul's
 Exhortations (3:1-18)**
 A. Request for Prayer (3:1-2)
 B. Strength needed for Steadfastness (3:3-5)
 C. Discipline the unruly, idle,
   and busybody (3:6-15)
 D. Blessing of peace and grace
   of Christ (3:16-18)

I. Faith, Persecution, and Glory (1:1-12)

1 Paul, Silas, and Timothy, to the Thessalonian church in God our Father and our Lord Jesus Christ: ²Grace to you and peace from God the Father and the Lord Jesus Christ.

³It is right for us always to give thanks to God for you, brothers and sisters, because of your abundantly growing faith, and increasing love of every one of you for one another. ⁴Therefore, we boast about you in the churches of God because of your endurance and faith in all the persecutions and afflictions in which you bear. ⁵This is confirmation of the righteous judgment of God—that you will be thought worthy of the kingdom of God, for which you are

suffering—⁶It is a just thing for God to
repay with affliction those who afflict you,
⁷and to give rest to you who are afflicted
and also to us, when the Lord Jesus is
revealed from heaven with his mighty
angels ⁸in flaming fire, inflicting full
vengeance on those who do not know God
and on those who do not obey the gospel
of our Lord Jesus. ⁹They will pay the
penalty of eternal destruction, away from
the face of the Lord and from the glory of
his might, ¹⁰when he comes on that day to
be glorified by his saints, and to be adored
by all of you who have believed, because of
our witness to you. ¹¹We always pray for
you that our God may make you worthy
of his calling and may power powerfully
fulfill every resolve for goodness and every
work of faith, ¹²so that the name of our
Lord Jesus may be glorified in you, and
you in him, according to the grace of our
God and of the Lord Jesus Christ.

A. Salutation (1:1-2)

Paul (with Timothy and Silas) opened this letter
with what would become his trademark expression
and the hallmark of a Christian. When Paul used
"grace and peace" to greet his readers, he did much
more than open a letter with a new Christian form
of greeting (1:2). If the readers were willing to listen
they would hear the voice of God speaking words
that ancient Israel's sages, prophets, priests, and kings

longed to hear. This ancient blessing was intended to lift the spirit and strengthen the heart of its recipient.

B. Fidelity Amid Persecution (1:3-10)

Paul needed to address a couple of important concerns, but first he wanted to encourage the Thessalonians. Their persecutions were a sign of courage. They showed that they were faithful. It was a demonstration of the depth and quality of love that they had for the Lord and for each other. Paul did not overlook this faithfulness, but pointed it out with authentic commendation. This act by Paul not only honored the faithful believers and showed any onlookers their genuineness, but brought glory to Christ (1:3-5). Paul urged them to stay strong and not let their guard down even for a minute, instead they were instructed to press on in excelling even more.

In the first letter to the Thessalonians, Paul prayed for their faith to increase and their love to abound. Here he affirmed that God was answering that prayer. Their faith was stronger and growing, and their love was even more evident. Thus, Paul heaped praise them for being receptive and proactive in response to his instructions, and to God's grace and work in their lives.[34]

C. The Glory of Christ at Work (1:11-12)

Paul spoke of the Thessalonians faithfulness as a part of Christ's glory.[35] Their attitude, with which they faced the trials and tribulations of life and the persecutors, served to show their sterling character and what God had worked in them. They received benefit from their faithfulness in times of persecution and their lives reflected the kingdom of God. Paul concluded that in their lives, the people around them could see the "visible" manifestation of God's presence (glory). That was serving to glorify Christ as their master-teacher. Jesus insisted, "But he that shall endure unto the end, the same shall be saved" (Matthew 24:13). Paul expressed that same idea here in commending them for their endurance as reflecting their inheritance in Jesus (5-12).[36]

For those who do not know God, the cost of sin will have to be paid. Paul depicted God as handing out the fruit of their rebellion against Him "on that day" as eternal destruction, which is their earned payment (see also Matthew 7:23). The Christians, who endure afflictions against them for Christ's sake, receive God's eternal reward of being with Christ forever (also 1 Thessalonians 4:17). This is a moment filled with the presence of God. For the faithful it is awe inspiring, for the persecutors of God's followers it is a time of vengeance, wrath, destruction, fear, and being cast away from the presence of God (11-12).[37]

II. Teaching on the End Times (2:1-17)

2 Now, brothers and sisters, in connection with the return of our Lord Jesus Christ, and our gathering together to him, we urge you ²not to be easily shaken out of your sanity, nor continue to be anxious, because a spirit, a prophetic word, or a letter pretending to be from us, said that the day of Lord has already come. ³Let no one deceive you in any way. For it will not be, unless the rebellion comes first, and the man of sin is revealed, the son of destruction, ⁴he who opposes and exalts himself against all that is called God or is sacred; so that he sits as God in the temple of God, proclaiming himself to be God. ⁵Don't you remember that I told you these things while I was with you? ⁶Now you know what holds him back so that he can be revealed when his time comes. ⁷The mystery of rebellion

is at work now, but is restrained until the one who is holding it back is out of the way. ⁸Then the rebel will be revealed. The Lord Jesus will destroy him with the breath from his mouth. When the Lord returns, his marvelous appearance will put an end to him. ⁹ When the rebel comes, it will happen through Satan's activity, with all kinds of counterfeit power, signs, and wonders. ¹⁰It will happen with every sort of wicked deception of those who are heading toward destruction, because they have refused to love the truth that would allow them to be saved. ¹¹For this reason, God confirms their delusion so that they trust their false belief. ¹²The result will be that everyone will be judged who is not convinced by the truth but delighted in unrighteousness.

¹³ But we must thank God always for you, brothers and sisters who are loved by God, because he chose you to be the first fruits of this salvation, through the sanctifying Spirit and through your faith in the truth. ¹⁴God called all of you through our gospel to obtain the glory of our Lord Jesus Christ. ¹⁵So then, brothers and sisters, stand firm and hold on to the traditions we taught you, both in person or through our letter. ¹⁶And now our Lord Jesus Christ himself and God our Father, who by grace loved us and gave us lasting comfort and a good hope, ¹⁷may he encourage your hearts and strengthen you in every good work that you do or good word that you say.

A. Day of the Lord's Return (2:1-3)

Paul needed to correct some errant rumors floating around in the church about Jesus' *Parousia*. It seemed some were thinking that Jesus was expected almost momentarily: like he was coming to dinner--tonight! In effect, Paul was saying, "Are you out of your mind!" But, this frantic stirring up of an erroneous belief was causing problems. Although Paul was probably expecting Jesus to return in Paul's lifetime, he realized that there was a lot of work to do before the end actually came. Also, there were some specific indicators that would signal the end was getting closer (also, see 1 Thessalonians 5:1-11 starting on page 33).

What Paul wanted to debunk quickly was the gossip that certain people had either gotten a letter from Paul, had talked secretly to him, or just had a "vision" indicating that Jesus had already returned. He had not! Do not believe it (2:1-3).

B. Rebellion and the Man of Sin (2:4-12)

Here he outlines why Jesus has not already returned. There is a revolt against God that is going to happen first. Although the images and specific details that Paul used are not known to us today, his first listeners would have understood his message. We may not know the exact details, but we cannot miss his main point, either. During the end times, there will be an obvious rebellion against God. During this time, a man of sin (literally, the lawless one) is going to be "revealed." He will claim to be "God;" however, he will be against everything for which the biblical God, as revealed in Jesus Christ, stands (2:4). Wickedness moves as a rising tide against God. This evil incarnate, who is masquerading as God, will meet the true God in the resurrected splendor of Jesus, and then be snuffed out (2:9).[38]

The most tragic part of this message is that all those who sided with the "man of sin" and joined his forces in the revolt will face God's righteous judgment, which carries destruction in its sentence (2:12).[39] This is a stern warning from Paul: Avoid this final destination!

C. Sanctification by the Spirit (2:13-15)

In contrast, Paul changed tones as he addressed the Thessalonian Church as faithful believers. His words of gentle, but firm rebuke, gave way to a synopsis of the Christian life. God took the initiative, that is, grace. God is the one who calls us through His seeking love. Otherwise, we could never respond, or seek God on our own.[40] God has not left us alone to save ourselves. God the Holy Spirit is at work in every human "heart seeking to awaken, convict, convert, and sanctify."[41] This is where God's grace and human response come together. God is calling, but who will answer?

In this short statement, Paul has the beginning and the end of salvation in view. He is giving them a quick look at the interconnected process by which God effects the work of grace in a Christian's life.

Certainly the Father has planned, and the Son has come, lived, died, was raised, and will come again. Between Christ's first advent and his *Parousia* (return), the work of the Holy Spirit is necessary in the life of every believer, sanctifying them, making them fit for the kingdom of God in heaven and also *currently* on earth. In order to obtain the glory of Christ to come, one must participate in God's present work in his or her heart and life (see 1 Thessalonians 5:23-24 starting on page 38).

Paul depicted the Thessalonians as among the first responders to the gospel of Christ, which he had been preaching (2:14). Paul made it clear that they were to abide by what he taught them and by what he reminded them of in this letter. He taught them the holy traditions, explained the gospel to them, and they were to get a firm grasp of these things in their lives (2:15).

D. Blessing of Encouragement (2:16-17)

The Thessalonians did not have to depend only on their own strength. Instead, God was providing the strength, hope, joy, and love. Paul reminded them of the continuity of God's faithful dealings in human affairs, especially with Israel, linked with salvation through Christ Jesus' salvific work, and applied to their hearts and lives by God's own Spirit. The triune activity of God is clearly seen in these verses. Here was enough evidence for them to commit their faith and hope. "Be of good courage, I have overcome..."

III. Paul's Exhortations (3:1-18)

3 In closing, brothers and sisters, pray for us that the message of the Lord may spread rapidly and gloriously, just as among you, ²and pray that we may be delivered from these perverse and wicked people, for not everyone has faith. ³But the Lord is faithful, and he will strengthen you and protect you from the evil one. ⁴We have confidence in the Lord that you are doing and will continue to do, the things we instruct. ⁵May the Lord direct your hearts in God's love and Christ's steadfastness.

⁶In the name of the Lord Jesus Christ, we instruct you, brothers and sisters, to keep back from every believer who behaves as a loafer and does not live according to the teaching you received from us. ⁷For you yourselves know how you ought to follow

our example. We were not idlers when we were with you, [8]nor did we eat anyone's food without paying for it. Instead, we labored and toiled night and day, so that we would not be a burden on any of you. [9]We did this, not because we do not have the right to such help, but we did this to offer ourselves as an example for you to imitate. [10]For even when we were with you, we gave you this instruction: "Whoever is unwilling to work shall not eat."

[11]We hear that some among you are behaving as loafers, doing no work, but being busybodies. [12]Such people we instruct and exhort in the Lord Jesus Christ to settle down and work for the food they eat. [13]Yet, as for you, brothers and sisters, never tire of doing what is good to help them. [14]However take special note of anyone who does not obey our instruction in this letter. Do not fellowship with them, in order that they may be shunned, [15]not regarded as an enemy, but reprimanded as a fellow believer.

[16]Now may the Lord of peace himself give you peace all the time and in every circumstance. The Lord be with all of you.

[17]This is how I, Paul, write my greeting in my own hand, which authenticates all my letters: [18]May the grace of our Lord Jesus Christ be with you all.

A. Request for Prayer (3:1-2)

Now Paul turns to the practical matters of appeal, urging, counsel, and encouragement arising out of the instructions and evidence previously given. One of the most fundamental Christian practices is prayer. This is a personal act of interactive spiritual formation in which the individual or group communicates with God. Prayer is an open avenue through which God works in the life of the believer and the whole Christian body. Paul prays "always" for them, and for others, and he believes that God will work through the prayers of his fellow Christians (1 Thessalonians 5:25, Romans 15:30ff, Philemon 22). For Paul, it was like breathing. Prayer flowed with his thoughts about them. He called upon them to participate in the work of the gospel with him by praying, too. We, also, ought to pray for one another always.

Paul wanted them to pray specifically for help with a difficult situation. By requesting prayer for this, he modeled what he taught. Once again, obstacles blocked Paul and he needed the church to take up the vigil in prayer. In this mystic sweet communion of prayer, God can meld hearts, build bonds of love, and release captives. We cannot enumerate all that God can do in prayer, but Paul was certain that God worked through the churches' prayers.

Paul highlighted a key stumbling block to the spread of the gospel in this short phrase, "but not all have faith." It is not because God is unwilling for them to have faith. God gives to each person a measure of faith (Romans 12:3). There is a tremendous responsibility associated with our ability to respond in faith. We can use it to open our hearts, or to close them off.[42] Faith's appeal is universal, but people can decline to use the faith they have. This tragedy of unbelief finally catches up with everyone who refuses God.

B. Strength Needed for Steadfastness (3:3-5)

It is not time to focus on the negative, so Paul lifts the mood of the letter to affirm that the Lord is dependable to strengthen them against the tricks of the evil one. The instructions that Paul laid down to guide them, have been reinforced by the Lord's own power to inspire their compliance and implementation (3:3-4). His prayer and assurance for them still applies to us today. "Best of all, God is with us," said John Wesley with his last few breaths. If we depend on the Lord, he will carry us through whatever we face. Thus we affirm, "I can do [endure] all things through Christ who gives me strength" (Philippians 4:13).

Paul invokes "God love" in verse 5. This is the kind of love that reaches out to someone, not expecting to gain something from them. It does not seek the other because of a lack in God. On the contrary, it is a self-giving love that brings freshness, strength, and renewal of character to the recipient. God's love at work in the believer is transformative. It forms, re-forms, and re-images the person to become like Christ. This is the kind of patient love that acts on our behalf even when we did not care: "While we were still sinners, Christ died for us" (Romans 5:8). It calls for a response to the originator of love, God, but also is linked on the horizontal plane with how we think, act, and speak toward others (3:5). Is it time to check how we love others compared to God?

C. Discipline the Unruly (3:6-15)

Jesus was a carpenter. Paul was a tentmaker. The Jewish work ethic did not allow an able-bodied person to just sit around collecting alms for their self-support. Even the rabbi or the scholar had to work with his hands. Paul had no easy words for the lazy "freeloaders" mooching off of their industrious and conscientious fellow believers. But, even more damage was being done to the Christian reputation of the church by gossipy behavior. Not only had some factions given up working to sit idly by and watch the skies, but they were spreading false rumors about others and meddling in their business. Paul calls them to a strict account, to repent of this behavior or be shunned by the community until they gave up those erroneous and sinful ways. They could not weasel out of this stern rebuke without being severed from the Christian community. Paul directs the Christian fellowship to discipline these unruly idlers for their own good, and for the work of the gospel. The world around us may not be following our Lord, but if they see a contrary, unloving, inconsistent life, they will not respect the Christian, the gospel message, or the Lord.

D. Blessing of Peace and Grace of Christ (3:16-18)

Paul closes this letter with the calm assurance that what he has said and prayed for concerning the Thessalonians would come to fruition and produce the hoped for fruit. The letter has had inspiringly positive high points and stern places of challenge and rebuke. However, because of God's powerful love, there was no waver in the confidence of what God would do in their lives.

The Thessalonians were suffering persecution; were mourning deceased friends and relatives; were troubled about the Lord's return. They were acquainted with the "mystery of rebellion." Others of their number were fainthearted; still others were lazy, neglectful, and financially draining on their friends.[43] Turmoil and tranquility were themes interwoven throughout this letter, but Paul would not leave them in the doldrums.

Alternatively, Paul wanted to bring home to the Thessalonians the reality of Christ's all-suficient peace, the peace of God that passes understanding. Their lives faced trying ordeals, but Christ's peace was adequate to meet every circumstance and continually guard their hearts. No situation need shake them. His grace is always ample. When Paul called for grace and peace to flood their lives, he immersed them into God's rich history of dealing faithfully with His followers. God's love endures forever.

They needed divine strength to live from day to day. Paul was praying for God's very best to attend them in every way and in every circumstance. He was praying for their lives to take on the wholeness characterized by the coming kingdom of God. Even the "disorderly walkers" (as Wesley would call them) to whom Paul addressed a corrective word, if they repented, could experience this deep settled peace that only God gives. It would characterize their lives and witness. Therefore, Paul commended his cherished Thessalonians to the care of Christ in the assurance that "He who began a good work in [them] would see it through to completion" (Philippians 1:6). Christ will do the same for us.

Christian
Formation
Exercises

Why Christian Formation Exercises?

Paul instructs the Thessalonians in these letters on how to live a genuine Christian life. He saw that the goal as a mature attitude, informed and formed by godly characteristics and traits that are evident in the life of Jesus Christ, the perfect human. Paul offered to his readers/listeners his best inspired understanding of how to avoid moral laxity, and to grow through discipline, especially urging Christian formation in heart holiness (I Thessalonians 5:23-24), even those who were facing persecution.

These first letters of Paul to the newly established churches give us a glimpse of what was on the hearts and minds of these early Christians. Just like the church of today, they needed to know how to live among others for God, conducting themselves in such a way to exemplify and create a peaceful, harmonious society, reflecting the godly principles of the Bible. The Christian way is learned in conversation with others, and with the Holy Spirit, who is at work in us and throughout creation.

Paul's letters to the Thessalonian Christians describes how to be a Christian, how to behave, how to deal with suffering, and what to anticipate from God. These questions are for meditation (careful reflective concentration and prayer) and practice. God extends an invitation to each reader to be a part of this exciting, growing community of faith who are growing by God's grace.

> [3]His divine power has given us everything we need for a godly life through our knowledge of him who called us by his own glory and goodness. [4]Through these he has given us his very great and precious promises, so that through them you may participate in the divine nature, having escaped the corruption in the world caused by evil desires. [5]For this very reason, make every effort to add to your faith goodness; and to goodness, knowledge; [6]and to knowledge, self-control; and to self-control, perseverance; and to perseverance, godliness; [7]and to godliness, mutual affection; and to mutual affection, love. (2 Peter 1:3-7, NIV)

Paul, in I Thessalonians 5:23-24, prays that this progression will produce the desired holy results and characteristics in each of their lives. God's desire for today's Christians has not changed. We still need to be spirit-filled, sanctified Christians, living out scriptural holiness in our world.

The Christian formation questions provided have three parts:

1) **Theme**, the subject of the lesson
2) **Read**, the focus scripture passage
3) **Sing**, worship opportunity related to the theme
4) **Reflect,** an idea to think about
5) **Internalize**, questions to apply the passage to your life
6) **Relate**, ways to ally the theme among Christians or the larger world
7) **Prayer**.

As you use these questions in your own journey, begin by praying and memorizing this Christian prayer for purity. Over the centuries, millions of Christians worldwide have prayed it to commit to the essence of what we also seek:

> Almighty God, unto whom all hearts are open, all desires known, and from whom no secrets are hid. Cleanse the thoughts of our hearts by the inspiration of thy Holy Spirit, that we may perfectly love you, and worthily magnify your holy name, through Christ our Lord. Amen. (*The Book of Common Prayer*, pg. 313)

Many of Paul's more elaborated doctrines in his other epistles show up here in an early form. Yet, he says more about his understanding of Christ's return within these two short books of the New Testament then elsewhere, while also giving the reader descriptions, warnings, advice, and inspiration concerning God's gracious dealing with his people.

UMH stands for the United Methodist Hymnal. CH stands for the Celebration Hymnal. If the hymn listed is pafound in hymnary.org (a listing of words and music to common hymns), then the link is provided.

Learning from 1 Thessalonians

Exercise I: Grace and Peace

Theme: The gospel comes in the power of the Holy Spirit showing God's favor and peace to everyone.

Read: 1 Thessalonians 1:1-3

Sing: "The Comforter Has Come" - CH#386, http://www.hymnary.org/hymn/CEL/page/382.

Reflect: What do the words *grace* and *peace* mean to you?

Paul's writes to these churches to convey to his readers the favor and completeness of the blessing of God referred to in Numbers 6:23-26.

Internalize: How does the Spirit connect these concepts in your life?

Relate: Find someone this week in the church or in the community that needs to hear or experience grace and peace and offer them words and actions that will convey it to them. During your prayers for that person listen to see if God would have you do more than a one-time act.

Prayer: Lord, reach forth your hand of grace and establish our hearts in peace that we may confidently walk under the smile of your blessing and represent you to those with whom we interact today. Amen.

Exercise II: Faith, Love, and Hope

Theme: Faith, Love, and Hope are Christ-like characteristics that must be produced in the life of true Christians.

Read: 1 Thessalonians 1:2-10

Sing: "Thou Hidden Love of God" - UMH #414, http://www.hymnary.org/media/fetch/138417.

Reflect: Paul talks a lot about "faith, love, and hope." What does each term mean to you?

Paul makes clear that God does not "play favorites." "God shows no partiality" (2:11). Everyone is guilty of sin, but God offers reconciliation to all through Jesus Christ.

Internalize: How does your life display faith, love, and hope? What role does each of these virtues play in your daily life (1:3)? What does it mean to be an exemplary believer (1:2-10)?

Relate: Who do you know that needs to experience faith, love, or hope? This week, reach out to two people who are of a different ethnicity than you and do something that conveys one of these virtues. If someone asks, "Why," explain that your act is one way that you are trying to demonstrate God's love.

Prayer: Lord, we believe your gospel. Give us true faith in our Lord Jesus Christ, and let your love be shed abroad in our hearts by your Holy Spirit, who is at work in us to produce every good thought, word and action. Be the Lord of every motion of our heart. Amen.

Exercise III: Tested Character

Theme: Christian need to learn to do the right actions,even in difficult situations.

Read: 1 Thessalonians 2:1-16

Sing: "Gloria Patria" - UMH #70 or #71, http://www.hymnary.org/media/fetch/136623.

Reflect: What does Paul mean by sharing his life with people?

Paul worked with his hands to make his own living, and could not be accused of "living off" of his converts. In fact, he through hi right actions, shared more than the gospel message; he gave himself to them.

Internalize: How does the gospel influence the way you share your life with others? Does the way you interact with others meet the standards found in Scripture?

Relate: Demonstrate gospel character in your dealings with others as you go about your work this week.

Prayer: By your mercy and grace, O Lord, strengthen our lives that we may avoid being deceived by lying and evil people, but be directed in the ways of truth. May all our actions be guided by your Holy Spirit. We worship and adore you, Father, Son, and Spirit, one God who reigns without rival. Amen.

Exercise IV: Faithfulness vs. Persecution

Theme: Christians need to stand firm in the faith even when facing maltreatment.

Read: 1 Thessalonians 2:17 – 3:13

Sing: "Find us Faithful" by Steve Green.

Reflect: What is persecution? Why is encouragement so important for those facing troubles?

Internalize: How do Paul's words affect the way you face your troubles? How important is giving and receiving encouragement to you (3:2)?

Relate: This week encourage someone who is facing troubles to continue being faithful and standing firm in their faith.

Remember, even Jesus needed encouragement to face his trials. (See Matthew 3:17)

Prayer: O Lord, strengthen us with your grace so that nothing will impede our progress toward you. In this dangerous world, keep us from losing our way or succumbing to those who would discourage us from following you. Let your protection and providence direct our way. Amen.

Exercise V: Called to Holiness of Life

Theme: The will of God for your sanctification (1 Thessalonains 4:3).

Read: 1 Thessalonians 4:1-12

Sing: "Called unto Holiness" - http://library.timelesstruths.org/music/Called_unto_Holiness/pdf/.

Reflect: Sin is incompatible with the Christian life. What sins has God freed you from, since you turned to Him? What still needs to be done (4:3-8)?

The Holy Spirit will lead us into all truth and holiness. His presence in our lives is to make us holy. The Holy Spirit is the fountain of all holiness for the Church-at-large and for its individual members. By His grace and virtue, our guilt is relieved and we are renewed in the image of the Creator. We must give His call to holiness our highest attention.

Internalize: What does it mean to control your own body in holiness? Have you ever felt God's love, the way Paul talks about it to the Thessalonians (4:9-12)?

Relate: Pray for the sanctification of a family member, friend, or neighbor.

Prayer: Send your Holy Spirit, O Father, to guide all my ways. Sanctify me and build me up in your holiness and love. Because of your Son, Jesus Christ, my Lord, may I be clothed in your holiness and found blameless. Amen

Exercise VI: Jesus is Coming—Again!

Theme: Be ready for Christ's return.

Read: 1 Thessalonians 4:13-5:11

Sing: "Lo! He Comes, with Clouds Descending" - UMH #718, http://www.hymnary.org/media/fetch/147838.

Reflect: What does the "day of the Lord" entail for believers and non-believers?

Internalize: How does knowing Jesus will come back make you feel? How does it affect your faith today (4:13-5:11)?

Relate: Discuss Jesus' return with your local church youth group.

Prayer: Most gracious Lord, fill us with a sense of anticipation to see your return. Likewise, help those who do not know you to repent and turn to you. Filled with your love, may we live obediently to you, and be prepared to rejoice in your return. Amen.

Exercise VII: Read the Bible and Pray

Theme: Christians should continually listen and talk with God (1 Thessalonains 5:17).

Read: 1 Thessalonians 5:12-22

Sing: "Thy Word is a Lamp unto my Feet" - UMH #840, http://www.hymnary.org/hymn/NHTB1891/page/466.

Reflect: What is the role of prayer in the Christian life? How often should I read the Bible? Do I sincerely mean all that I am praying? Do I seek the Spirit's assistance to pray about the right things? Do I pray for faith, hope, and love to increase in my life? In the church? Do I have a regular time for prayer? Do I pray for God's purpose or my own? Do I pray for other's needs?

If you want to know what God's plan is, read the Bible. God will also talk with him in prayer. Sir William Temple (1628 - 1699) remarked about prayer, "When I pray, coincidences happen, and when I don't, they don't."

Internalize: How do prayer and Bible reading help you in your walk with God (5:16-18)? How has prayer and biblical instruction by the church affected your walk with the Lord (5:12-22)?

Relate: Talk to two people about the importance of the Bible and the place of prayer in their lives. Pray for the protection of all Christians in harm's way.

Prayer: Give me strength, O Lord, and assist me when I pray. Reveal yourself through your Word, so that through the Holy Spirit I might better understand your will. Allow my prayers to reflect both your will for my life and your desire to love others more.

Exercise VIII: Entire Sanctification

Theme: Love should rule the Christian's heart.

Read: 1 Thessalonians 5:23-24

Sing: "Take my Life and Let it be consecrated, Lord, to Thee" - UMH #399, http://www.hymnary.org/media/fetch/96019.

Reflect: What does it mean to belong totally to God? What is the role of the Holy Spirit in the work of entire sanctification? Can we be sanctified entirely? Where does love fit in this discussion?

Genuine love gives the whole self—God to us, us to God. When love is enthroned in the heart, one's alignment with the will and mission of God becomes single-minded. This personal heart-felt commitment stands behind the mission of Christian evangelism, discipleship, catechesis, life, and lifestyle.

Internalize: In your life, what is the importance of being Entirely Sanctified? (5:23-24) Why is this so important? How is this evident in your life? How can God use you for the work of ministry among believers? Out in the community?

Relate: How evident is entire sanctification in the life of your local Christian fellowship? Can you give examples? In what ways does your church use its godly spiritual presence to serve in the community?

Prayer: O God, the God of peace, sanctify me entirely. May my whole spirit, soul and body be kept blameless at the coming of our Lord Jesus Christ. I know you are faithful and will do it. Praise you! Thank you! Amen

Learning from 2 Thessalonians

Exercise IX: Facing Opposition

Theme: Christians have to endure persecution and affliction.

Read: 2 Thessalonians 1:3-10

Sing: "What a Friend We Have in Jesus" - UMH #526, http://www.hymnary.org/media/fetch/144065.

Reflect: How does a Christian define persecution and affliction? What spiritual practices does Paul suggest to relieve these troubles?

Internalize: How do Paul's answers apply to your life? In what ways have you faced persecution in your life because of being a faithful Christian? How did God help you in the situation (1:3-10)?

Relate: If possible, stand with someone in trouble, especially helping them through the situation by doing the right thing. Pray for Christians facing persecution.

Pray: O Lord, give strength to all those who are in distress, or struggle with pain, poverty, affliction, or persecution. Forgive those who do evil against us and bring them to repentance for their deeds. Give us your joy that we may be strong in the Lord no matter what we face. Amen.

Exercise X: The Lord's Return

Theme: Jesus is coming back to earth to reign.

Read: 2 Thessalonians 2:1-12

Sing: "Christ, Whose Glory Fills the Skies" - UMH #173, http://www.hymnary.org/hymn/UMH/page/173.

Reflect: Where will Jesus reign? What will it be like? What will be absent? Who will participate in it?

It seemed that some believers were thinking that Jesus was coming back any minute, as if he was coming to dinner--tonight! Paul had to correct these rumors floating around the church about Jesus' return.

Internalize: How does the Lord's return affect your faith, and life? Are you excited? Nervous? Ambivalent (2:1-3)? What do you have to do to be ready for Jesus' return?

Relate: Help someone understand the true meaning and purpose of Jesus' second coming.

Pray: Lord, Help us to be good stewards of the time we have on this earth before you come back. Let us live each day as faithful servants of your coming kingdom. Change our hearts, our homes, churches, and communities to reflect your truth, justice, and holiness. Amen.

Exercise XI: Constancy of Christ

Theme: The Lord is dependable in all things.

Read: 2 Thessalonians 3:3-5

Sing: "Trust and Obey" - UMH #467, http://www.hymnary.org/media/fetch/138917.

Reflect: How can we depend on God? What role does prayer play in trusting God (3:1-2)?

Internalize: Christ is a steady constant in the life of believers. How has this proved true in your life (3:3-5)? Christian discipline is important to help us be consistent Christians. How has the church helped you be more consistent (3:6-15)?

Relate: Tell someone this week one event where you saw the Lord's faithfulness in your life.

Pray: Father, thank you for being someone we can depend on. Through Christ's work on the cross you sent the Holy Spirit to be your constant abiding presence with us each day. God for your faithfulness we offer to you endless praise. Amen.

Further considerations from 2 Thessalonians

1) What does it mean for the "Glory of Christ" to be at work in you (1:11-12)?

2) What does Paul say about those who reject the grace of God and choose rebellion (2:4-12)?

3) What is the importance of allowing the Holy Spirit to sanctify you (2:13-15)?

4) How has encouragement from the church affected your walk with the Lord (2:16-17)?

5) Paul opens and closes his letters with references to "grace and peace." What do these experiences mean tl you (3:16-17)?

When King Jesus Comes Back to Earth to Reign

We are praying for the coming
of Christ's unending day,

When He shall restore the world in
His grand own peaceful way.
All the earth is groaning, crying for
that Day of perfect peace—

When King Jesus comes back to earth to reign.

Knowledge of the Lord shall fill the
whole earth, sea, and sky,
When Jesus' coming back again
answers all earth's cries.
God shall wipe away each tear
from our weeping eyes,

When King Jesus comes back to earth to reign.

The ransomed of the Lord shall
come to Zion filled with joy,
And in all His holy mountain, no one
will sorrow, hurt, or destroy.
Perfect love will adorn every heart, and
His peace hold righteous sway,

When King Jesus comes back to earth to reign.

—R.J. Hiatt

Benediction

Almighty and everlasting God, we lift up our hearts to you for your keeping. By your eternal Son we come into your presence through your loving Holy Spirit. Inspire us to be faithful to you all our days, and walk in mercy and justice before our brothers and sisters in this world. Help us conduct all our thoughts, words, and works according to your love as shown in Jesus Christ our Lord for your glory. May we walk humbly before you and fulfill our purpose in your everlasting kingdom, today, and every day of our lives. Amen.

Notes

1. Salonika, or Thessaloniki as it is called today, is the second largest City in Greece with a population of about 394,000 (2011).

2. They could appoint their own local governing leaders.

3. Xerxes the Persian King (fl. 480 BC) invaded Europe from there.

4. Eerdman, p. 9.

5. Moffatt, p. 23.

6. Moffatt, p. 3.

7. First Thessalonians is found in Marcion's canon, the Muratorian canon, and is quoted by name by Irenaeus, Clement of Alexandria, Tertullian, indicating very early acceptance as being authentic.

8. Airhart, p. 435.

9. Bruce, p. 11

10. Bruce, p.11.

11. Miller, p. 160.

12. The New Testament is composed of 27 documents (books) of which 21 are letters (called epistles). Paul's

name is associated with 13 of them. Nine of these letters were written to young churches, new Christians.

13. Long, p. 5. This style of argumentation is called *epicheireme*. He explains further, "there is a fairly consistent pattern of a pair of premises and proofs (often with gar) followed by a conclusion (often with an inferential Greek particle like *oun*). Noteworthy is the fact that a large majority of the conclusions reached contain a direct exhortation to "live morally" arising out of the preceding argument (1 Thessalonians 4:18; 5:6, 11; 2 Thessalonians 2:15; 1 Corinthians 4:5, 16; 5:4-5, 8, 13; 8:13; Romans 6:11-12; Acts 17:29; 20:31, 35) or an indirect appeal to live morally (1 Thessalonians 4:8, 10b; Romans 6:4, 21-22; 7:4)" (p.22). I will give attention to Long's thesis in the above highlighted sections.

14. Winter, p. 70.

15. The longer form of his name is Silvanus.

16. These terms are used specifically to let them know of the favor and wholeness to be found in God.

17. Shekinah, (הניבש; literally, "the dwelling"), is taken from biblical texts that speak of "God dwelling" either in the Tabernacle or among the people of Israel (cf. Exodus 25:8, 29:45-46; Numbers 5:3, 35:34; I Kings 4:13; Ezekiel 43:9; Zechariah 2:14).

18. Dunning, p. 405, 407, 409.

19. The plural Greek word *adelphoi* (literally, "brothers") in the New Testament, may refer to men, or to both men and women siblings, thus (brothers and sisters). In God's family, the church, we are all siblings.

20. Barclay, p. 187.

21. Airhart, p. 441.

22. Airhart, p. 461.

23. Paul makes the clear connection of Jesus and the Father. Paul means for his readers to understand that God is meant when he refers to either one. Jesus is not the Father, but is, however, God.

24. Eucharistian, the Greek word for thanks used here, carries this celebrative notion of grace present in the Lord's Supper event into their lives, joining them in fellowship and heart.

25. This may refer to angels, "saints," or "holy ones." See Deuteronomy 33:2; Daniel 7:10; Zechariah 14:5; Mark 8:38, for example.

26. Bruce, p. 30.

27. Some other pertinent references are OT: Exodus 20:14; Leviticus 18:20; Deuteronomy 5:18, 22:22-24; Isaiah 23:17; Jeremiah 3:8; Ezekiel 16:26; NT: Matthew 5:31-32, 15:19, 19:9; Hebrews 13:4, Jude 7; Revelation 17:2.

28. Paul was not teaching directly about a doctrine of God, Jesus, and the Holy Spirit, as he wrote about these other matters of Christian conduct, but he wove together the being and work of the Father, Christ, and the Holy Spirit into a united whole who think and act as One, yet with characteristic (but not isolated) roles. He does not elaborate on this in 1 Thessalonians, but it is still a present reality (see 1:1, 9-10, 14; 3:11; 4:8; 5:23).

29. Dunning, p. 426.

30. Dunning, p. 426.

31. Dunning notes (p. 512-13) that the concept, Day of the Lord, was familiar to the ancient Jews. But, the prophets like Amos (5:18-27) and Jeremiah (chapters

7 and 26) interpreted it as to also condemn a self-centered institutionalism preoccupied with its own national treasure, success, or shrine (the Temple) over God's mission, that would fall under the same judgment and destruction. The nation of Israel was not exempted! It still isn't.

32. See John Wesley's *Plain Account of Christian Perfection* for a detailed delineating of this concept.

33. Bruce, p. 33.

34. Morris, p. 114.

35. Glory and kingdom are key terms that we need to understand. Paul uses kingdom rarely, but it can refer to the "active rule of God" in the life of Christians, like Jesus mainly used it (Romans 14:17—and a key for understanding Wesley on this point; 1 Corinthians 4:20; Colossians 1:13). Paul also used it to mean the future eschatological age (1 Corinthians 6:9ff; Galatians 5:21; 2 Thessalonians 1:5), and has a "place" in mind. His glory is the weight of his awesome presence, particularly seen in the life, death, resurrection, and ascension of Christ manifest fully in his enthroned kingship (2 Corinthians 4:4-6). In a secondary sense, it refers to things associated with God, or people with whom he shares in presence (ascribe: Romans 4:20, 11:36; 2 Corinthians 1:20), (eschatological significance: Mark 13:26; Matthew 25:31; 1 Peter 4:13), (share in: Romans 5:2, 8:18; et. all), (raised in: 1 Corinthians 15:43).

36. Best, p. 249.

37. Best, p.263.

38. Airhart, p. 519.

39. Guthrie, p. 858. Guthrie points out that Paul in 2 Thessalonians 1:5, 2 Timothy 4:8, and Romans 2:5 saw

the concepts of God's judgment being the outcome of God's righteous justice and these are tied to the day of wrath. Those who follow the man of sin will perish (2 Thessalonians 2:10), and suffer thoroughly deserved destruction (Romans 2:12). Airhart also suggests this same understanding can be found in Isaiah 5:20, or heard in Exodus 9:7, 12 and 2 Chronicles 18:22. See also Romans 1:18-32 (p. 521).

40. Barclay, p. 214.

41. Greathouse, p. 54. This is essentially John Wesley's understanding and teaching on "prevenient" grace.

42. Barclay, p. 216.

43. Airhart, p. 534.

Works Cited

Airhart, Arnold E. *I and II Thessalonians*. Vol. 9, in *Galatians through Philemon*, Beacon Bible Commentary. Kansas City, MO: Beacon Hill Press, 1964-1969.

"The Letter to the Philippians, Colossians, and Thessalonians." In *The Daily Study Bible*, by William Barclay, 187. Philadelphia: Westminster Press, 1975.

Bruce, F. F. *Paul and His Converts; 1 and 2 Thessalonians, 1 and 2 Corinthians*, Bible Guides. Vol. 17. London: Lutterworth Press, 1965.

Dunning, H. Ray. *Grace, Faith, and Holiness: A Wesleyan Systematic Theology*. Kansas City, MO: Beacon Hill Press of Kansas City, 1988.

Erdman, Charles Rosenbury. *The Epistles of Paul to the Thessalonians: An Exposition*. Philadelphia: Westminster Press, 1935.

Ernest, Best. *A Commentary on the First and Second Epistles to the Thessalonians*, Harper's New Testament Commentaries. New York: Harper & Row, 1972.

The Episcopal Church . (2007). *The Book of Common Prayer*. (G. M. Howe, Ed.) New York: Church Publishing Incorporated.

Greathouse, William M., and H. Ray Dunning. *An Introduction to Wesleyan Theology*. Kansas City, MO: Beacon Hill Press of Kansas City, 1982.

Guthrie, Donald. *New Testament Theology*. Downers Grove, IL: Inter-Varsity Press, 1981.

Holy Bible, New International Version (NIV). (1973, 1978, 1984, 2011). Biblica, Inc. Used by permission. All rights reserved worldwide.

Long, Fredrick J. "From Epicheiremes to Exhortation: A Pauline Method for Moral Persuasion in 1 Thessalonians." In *Rhetoric, Ethic, and Moral Persuasion in Biblical Discourse: Essays from the 2002 Heidelberg Conference*, by Thomas H. Olbricht and Anders Eriksson, 179-195. New York: T & T Clark International, 2005.

Miller, Adam William. *An Introduction to the New Testament*. Anderson, Ind. : Warner Press, 1961, 1943.

Moffatt, James. *The First and Second Epistles to the Thessalonians*. Vol. 4, in *The Expositor's Greek Testament*, by W. Robertson, Sir Nicoll, 3-54. London: Hodder and Stoughton, 1897-1910. https://archive.org/details/expositorsgreekt04nicouoft (accessed January 23, 2014)

Morris, Leon. *The Epistles of Paul to the Thessalonians: An Introduction and Commentary*, Tyndale New Testament Commentaries. Edited by R. V. G. Tasker. Vol. 13. Grand Rapids, MI: William B. Eerdmans Publishing Co., 1984.

Wesley, John. *A Plain Account of Christian Perfection*. New York: Carlton & Porter, 1866?

Winter, Bruce W. "Secular and Christian Responses to Corinthian Famines." *Tyndale Bulletin* 40, no. 1 (1989): 86-106. http://98.131.162.170//tynbul/library/TynBull_1989A_40_05_Winter_CorinthianFamines.pdf (accessed January 23, 2014)

Images Cited

These images have been turned to gray scale and modified slightly for print and eReader formats. To view the original images, in color, please visit the website in the citation.

Image 1 on page 2: "Overview of Geography Relevant to Paul of Tarsus." *Wikipedia.* December 11, 2012. http://en.wikipedia.org/wiki/File:Broad_overview_of_geography_relevant_to_paul_of_tarsus.png (accessed January 21, 2014). This file is licensed under the Creative Commons Attribution-Share Alike 3.0 Unported license.

Image 2 on page 3: "Kassander King of Macedonia Kingdom of Greece Stater." *Wikipedia.* January 16, 2014. http://en.wikipedia.org/wiki/File:Kassander_king_of_Macedonia_kingdom_of_greece.jpg (accessed January 22, 2013). This file is licensed under the Creative Commons Attribution-Share Alike 2.5 Generic license.

Image 3 on page 4: Rembrandt. "Apostle Paul." *Wikipedia.* October 28, 2008. http://en.wikipedia.org/wiki/File:Rembrandt_Harmensz._van_Rijn_163.jpg (accessed January 21, 2014).

Image 4 on page 5: "Mt. Olympus." *Holy Land Photos*. Carl Rasmussen. July 13, 2008. http://holylandphotos.org/browse.asp?s =1,4,13,31,283,285&img=GNMTTHCT01 (accessed January 22, 2014).

Image 5 on page 9: "Forum/Agora 3." *Holy Land Photos*. Carl Rasmussen. September 1, 2011. http://holylandphotos.org/browse.asp?s= 1,4,13,31,283,284&img=GNMTTH54 (accessed January 21, 2014).

Image 6 on page 10: Asbury Theological Seminary Archives. "Colossians 4:14-18 and 1 Thessalonians 1:1-13, 1598 Geneva Bible." ePlace Images From the Archives. http://place.asburyseminary.edu/ fromthearchives/5/ (accessed February 21, 2014). Image in the public domain.

Image 7 on page 12: Asbury Theological Seminary Archives. "Colossians 4:7-19 and 1 Thessalonians 1:1-8, Codex Vaticanus B." ePlace Images From the Archives. http://place.asburyseminary.edu/ fromthearchives/2/ (accessed February 20, 2014). Image in the public domain.

Image 8 on page 25: "Saint Timothy." *Wikipedia*. March 22, 2008. http://en.wikipedia.org/wiki/File:Saint_ Timothy.jpg (accessed February 21, 2014). Image in the public domain.

Image 9 on page 42: Asbury Theological Seminary Archives. "1 Thessalonians 4:15-5:28 and 2 Thessalonians 1:1-4, 1598 Geneva Bible." ePlace Images From the Archives. http://place. asburyseminary.edu/fromthearchives/4/ (accessed February 21, 2014). Image in the public domain.

Image 10 on page 44: Asbury Theological Seminary Archives. "2 Thessalonians 3:11-18 and Hebrews 1:1-2:2, Codex Vaticanus B." ePlace Images From the Archives. http://place.asburyseminary.edu/fromthearchives/1/ (accessed February 21, 2014). Image in the public domain.

www.ingramcontent.com/pod-product-compliance
Lightning Source LLC
Chambersburg PA
CBHW061750020426
42331CB00006B/1422